The HCG Diet

Creative Phase 3 HCG Diet Meal Ideas

All Rights Reserved. No part of this publication may be reproduced in any form or by any means, including scanning, photocopying, or otherwise without prior written permission of the copyright holder. Copyright © 2014

Table of Contents
Introduction
Why the HCG Diet?
Foods to Avoid
Recipes
- **Simple Chicken Matzo Ball Soup**
- **Zucchini Fries**
- **Bacon Wrapped Brussels Sprouts**
- **Slow Cooker Collard Greens**
- **All-Day Meatball Marinara**
- **Natural Italian Chicken Sausage**
- **No-Bun Bacon Burger**
- **Apple Cinnamon Waffles**
- **Kelp Noodle Stir-Fry**
- **Quick Beanless Chili**
- **Macadamia Crusted Ahi Tuna**
- **Parchment Baked Salmon**
- **Seafood Paella**

- Zucchini Salad with Sundried Tomato Sauce
- Cashew Crunch Kelp Noodle Salad
- Raspberry Almond Salad
- Healthy Chicken Satay
- Oven-Fried Chicken
- Baked Egg Muffins
- Spicy Kale with Poached Eggs
- Spicy Oregano Cubes
- Red Pepper Chicken Fries
- Chicken Bruschetta
- Salmon with Berry Chutney
- Baked Tilapia Filets
- Mushroom Masala
- Ground Beef Stuffed Peppers
- Chicken Souvlaki Kebobs
- Homestyle Meatloaf
- Asian Empanada

Introduction

So you have finally gotten through that boring phase 2 of the HCG diet and you're excited about starting phase 3? This book will help you transition smoothly and make good food choices. The third phase of this diet plan will allow you a greater choice of foods with which you can create delicious recipes. It should be greatly rewarding after the monotony of the second phase! In phase 3, you can experiment with different foods and create yummy recipes that will make it much easier to stick with this very important phase. This book contains 30 mouth-watering all-natural recipes for phase 3 of the HCG diet. In fact, these recipes will even be appreciated by your family members who are not on the HCG diet!

These recipes feature healthy fats, nuts, meat, eggs, veggies and fruits such as berries and apples. Traditional starches such as pasta, bread and rice are replaced by grated cauliflower, lettuce leaves or kelp noodles for nutritious low-starch, low-carb or low-sugar options that are perfect for the HCG diet's third phase.

Why the HCG Diet?

The HCG Diet is a controversial diet plan that involves receiving injections of a synthetic hormone known as human chorionic gonadotropin (HCG), a hormone naturally produced by women's bodies during pregnancy. This hormone, when paired with an extremely low calorie diet (500 calories per day on average) is thought to help with rapid weight loss, particularly in stubborn areas such as arms, thighs and stomach. Sometimes, HCG is taken in the form of pellets or droplets. Spray

The HCG hormone works by releasing fat from storage and making it available for use as fuel by the body. Circulating fat is extremely high in calories, hence the very low calorie diet that accompanies the hormone treatment. The food eaten on the HCG plan serves as a source of essential nutrients. Most people report feeling less hungry after a few days, once their body becomes accustomed to using stored fat as fuel.

There are several different HCG diet plans, but they all follow the same principles: eliminate alcohol, starches and carbs, sugar as well as processed foods and prioritize lean meats, organic produce and fish. Usually, this diet is best followed under medical supervision because it may not be safe for everyone. Most HCG dieters will have two small meals per day, consisting of one protein, one "carb", one fruit and one veggie. The allowed carbs are either one dry breadstick or a Melba toast. Obviously, this isn't gluten-free-friendly.

The HCG diet plan must be followed closely in order to see the benefits. This means that you can't substitute your dry breadstick for an extra apple, you must eat the breadstick. It is also not recommended to eat the same meat twice in the same day. This means that if you choose chicken for your first meal, you should have broiled salmon or lean beef for the other meal. This ensures a relative balance of nutrients since a very low calorie diet struggles to provide all the recommended essential nutrients if not planned properly.

The HCG diet is said to be very effective for some people, who have successfully lost 1-2 pounds a day. However, the controversy surrounding it makes some doctors hesitant to prescribe HCG shots to someone who wishes to lose weight. HCG shots for weight loss are currently not approved by the FDA, and there is a lack of strong studies that indicate the benefits and safety of this diet. Still, many people try it and enjoy its benefits on their figure.

Like many other popular diet plans, the HCG diet contains 4 phases which are designed to potentialize fat loss. The first phase is optional and simply consists of choosing natural foods and doing cleanses that might be beneficial once the protocol starts. It can be skipped with no detrimental effects. The second phase is the bulk of the HCG diet. On the first two days of phase 2, you need to stuff yourself with fatty foods to build up reserves for the upcoming challenge. Starting on the third day, you need to eat 500 calories' worth of specific "allowed" foods per day. The list is pretty short and restrictive, and can easily be found online or through a diet coach. This phase lasts a month on average, and turbo charges your body into fat burning mode.

The third phase is where you start your recovery, and is arguably the most important phase. A greater variety of foods is allowed, along with the possibility to make some delicious recipes. This is where this cookbook comes in with its delicious phase 3-friendly recipes. The Melba toast you had to eat in phase 2 is no longer allowed. The goal of phase 3 is to stabilize your weight and reintroduce foods into your diet. Starches and sugar must still be avoided at all costs, and this includes high-sugar fruits like bananas and grapes.

The last phase is maintenance, which consists of eating normally but healthy. You reintroduce all foods very slowly while taking note of their effect on your weight. Some people don't tolerate starches and sugar or other foods and must avoid them during maintenance. Maintenance usually lasts for the rest of your life, unless you decide to do another round of HCG after several weeks of maintenance.

Since eating a piece of plain broiled chicken, a Melba toast, an apple and celery sticks every day may lose its appeal after a while, it will be very exciting to enter phase 3. The key is moderation and variety. Note that all the recipes in this book are additionally Paleo-friendly and gluten-free. You can simply add anything that's missing on the side to create a complete phase 3 HCG diet meal.

Additional tips: Make sure you calculate your portion sizes to avoid busting your calorie budget. If you need to eat 1000 calories or less on phase 3, it cannot be 1100. Most of these recipes will make more than one HCG-friendly serving, so you can store it in the refrigerator and eat it the next day, or share it with someone. Avoid eating leftovers the same night because of the nutrient balance issue discussed earlier.

Foods to Avoid

In phase 3, you will need to avoid:

- Beans of all types
- Soda pop
- Alcohol in excess (can be consumed in moderation, such as one glass of wine with dinner)
- Artificially flavored and sweetened "water enhancers" such as Crystal Light
- Meat with visible fat or skin (bacon can be eaten in moderation)
- High calorie foods (chips, candy, chocolate and other junk food)
- Carbs and starches (rice, bread, potatoes, grains, pasta, etc.)
- Most dried fruits
- Starchy fruits such as bananas
- High-sugar fruits such as mangoes, grapes and cherries
- High-fat fruits such as avocadoes
- High-sugar or starchy veggies such as carrots, plantains, corn, beets and peas
- All forms of sugar (honey, table sugar, molasses, maple sugar, agave nectar, etc. Stevia is allowed, but NOT artificial sweeteners.)

Note that all the fruits and veggies on this list are not expressly forbidden by the original HCG diet and can be consumed in small amounts (think one dried date or a quarter cup of corn). However, they are easily avoided and should be whenever possible.

Simple Chicken Matzo Ball Soup

Prep Time: 15 minutes*

Cook Time: 30 minutes

Servings: 4

INGREDIENTS

16 oz (1 lb) chicken pieces

2 cups chicken stock (or vegetable stock)

1 cup almond flour

2 cage-free egg yolks

Pinch ground white pepper (or ground black pepper)

3/4 teaspoon Celtic sea salt

INSTRUCTIONS

1. In a medium mixing bowl, beat eggs, salt and pepper until light and frothy, about 2 minutes. Sift almond flour into bowl and mix until dough comes together.
2. *Cover dough with parchment, if preferred, and refrigerate 2 - 4 hours.
3. Heat medium pot over medium heat. Add 1 teaspoon salt to large pot of water and bring to boil.
4. Place chicken in hot pot skin-side down. Brown chicken on all sides, about 15 minutes.
5. Remove dough from refrigerator and roll into balls. Carefully place dough balls in boiling water. Reduce heat to low, cover and simmer 20 minutes, until cooked through.

6. Add chicken too browned chicken stock. Cook about 15 minutes. Remove chicken and chop, then add back to pot.
7. Transfer matzo balls to serving dish with slotted spoon. Ladle heated chicken stock over matzo balls and serve hot.

Zucchini Fries

Prep Time: 15 minutes

Cook Time: 15 minutes

Servings: 2

INGREDIENTS

1 medium zucchini

1 cage-free egg

1/2 cup almond meal

1 teaspoon flax meal (or ground chia seed)

1/2 teaspoon paprika

1 teaspoon ground black pepper

1 teaspoon Celtic sea salt

Coconut oil (for cooking)

INSTRUCTIONS

1. Cut zucchini in half, then slice into 1/3 inch strips. Sprinkle with 1/2 teaspoon salt and place between paper towels to drain excess water. Set aside 10 minutes.
2. Heat large pan over medium-high heat and coat with coconut oil.
3. In a shallow dish, blend almond meal, flax or chia meal, and remaining spices and salt. Beat egg in small mixing bowl.
4. Gently press paper towel to absorb excess moisture from zucchini.
5. In batches, toss zucchini strips in beaten egg to lightly coat, then dredge in seasoned almond meal.

6. Carefully place coated zucchini strips into hot oil and fry about 2 minutes per side, until golden brown and heated through. Turn with tongs half way through cooking.
7. Remove from pan and drain fried on paper towel. Transfer to serving dish.
8. Serve hot with your favorite sauce.

Bacon Wrapped Brussels Sprouts

Prep Time: 10 minutes

Cook Time: 20 minutes

Servings: 4

INGREDIENTS

24 Brussels sprouts

8 strips nitrate-free bacon

24 wooden toothpicks

1/4 teaspoon ground black pepper

INSTRUCTIONS

1. Preheat oven to 375 degrees F. Place oven-safe wire rack in sheet pan.
2. Soak toothpicks in water for about 5 minutes.
3. Cut bacon strips into thirds. Wrap each Brussels sprout in bacon and use toothpicks to secure.
4. Place bacon wrapped Brussels sprouts on wire rack and sprinkle with pepper.
5. Bake for about 15 - 20 minutes, until bacon is crisp and veggies are cooked through. Remove and let cool about 2 minutes.
6. Serve warm or room temperature.

Slow Cooker Collard Greens

Prep Time: 15 minutes

Cook Time: 6 hours

Servings: 6

INGREDIENTS

2 heads fresh collard greens or (2 large bags)

4 oz nitrate-free bacon (or 1 bone-in ham)

4 cups chicken stock (or broth)

Water

INSTRUCTIONS

1. Add bacon or ham hock to slow cooker. Cover with lid and turn on to high. Cook and render down about 30 minutes.
2. Rinse collards well and roughly chop. Place in large colander or in clean sink to drain.
1. Add enough greens to fill slow cooker. Reserve excess greens. Add 2 cups chicken stock.
2. Cover slow cooker with lid. Reduce temperature to medium and cook about 1 hour.
3. Add enough remaining greens to fill slow cooker. Add remaining chicken stock. Reserve any excess greens. Cook another hour.
4. Add any remaining greens to slow cooker. Cook another 3 hours, until tender.
5. Turn off slow cooker and carefully remove lid. Remove pork.
6. Transfer to serving dish and serve hot.

All-Day Meatball Marinara

Prep Time: 20 minutes

Cook Time: 4 hours

Servings: 4

INGREDIENTS

24 oz (1 1/2 lbs) ground meat (ground beef, pork, turkey, or any combination)

1/2 cup almond meal (or finely ground almonds)

2 cage-free eggs

2 cans (15 oz) organic tomato sauce

1 can (15 oz) organic crushed tomatoes

1/4 cup nutritional yeast (optional)

1 small onion (yellow or white)

2 garlic cloves

1 bay leaf

2 sprigs fresh basil

3 teaspoons dried oregano

2 teaspoons dried parsley

1 teaspoon dried basil

1/2 teaspoon onion powder

1/2 teaspoon garlic powder

1 teaspoon Celtic sea salt

1 tablespoon coconut oil (for cooking)

1 small bunch fresh flat-leaf Italian parsley (for garnish)

INSTRUCTIONS

1. Heat large skillet over medium-high heat. Add coconut oil to hot pan.
2. Peel onion and cut in half. Finely grate one half and add to medium mixing bowl. Reserve second half. Peel and mince garlic. Add half to mixing bowl. Reserve second half.
3. Add ground meat to medium mixing bowl with 1/4 cup tomato sauce, almond meal, eggs, 1 teaspoon dried oregano, 1 teaspoon dried parsley, onion powder, garlic powder, 1/2 teaspoon salt, and nutritional yeast (optional). Mix until well combined.
4. Form mixture into medium-sized meat balls. Add to hot oiled pan in batches and brown on all sides, about 5 minute per batch. Set aside in slow cooker.
5. Finely chop remaining onions. Add to hot oiled pan with garlic. Sauté about 5 minutes.
6. Add remaining tomato sauce, crushed tomatoes, 2 teaspoons dried oregano, 1 teaspoon dried parsley, 1/2 teaspoon salt, bay leaf, and fresh torn basil leaves. Stir and bring to simmer, about 5 minutes. Pour sauce over meatballs and stir to combine.
7. Cover slow cooker with lid. Turn on to low and cook 4 - 5 hours, until meatballs are cooked through.
8. Turn off slow cooker and carefully remove lid. Transfer to serving dish.
9. For garnish, chop fresh parsley and sprinkle over dish.
10. Serve hot.

Natural Italian Chicken Sausage

Prep Time: 5 minutes

Cook Time: 10 minutes

Servings: 4

INGREDIENTS

20 oz (1 1/4 lb) chicken (ground meat or whole pieces)

1/2 teaspoon all spice

1 teaspoon fennel seed

1 teaspoon ground sage

1 teaspoon dried thyme

1 teaspoon ground black pepper

1 teaspoon Celtic sea salt

Natural or synthetic sausage casing (optional)

Piping or kitchen bag (optional)

Coconut oil (for cooking)

INSTRUCTIONS

1. Heat medium skillet over medium heat and lightly coat with coconut oil.
2. Remove chicken skin and bones from pieces and coarsely grind in food processor, high-speed blender or meat grinder, if using.
3. Add ground chicken to medium mixing bowl with salt and spices and mix well.
4. Use meat grinder to stuff mixture into casing. Or scoop mixture into piping bag with no tip or kitchen bag with 1 inch corner cut

off, and pipe into casing. Twist casing tightly in opposite directions to section off 4-inch links while stuffing.
5. Or form into 8 - 12 round patties with hands.
6. Place links or patties in hot oiled skillet. Cook links about 4 - 5 minutes per side, until golden brown and cooked through. Or cook patties about 3 - 4 minutes per side, until golden brown and crisp. Turn halfway through cooking.
7. Drain cooked sausage on paper towel. Serve hot.

No-Bun Bacon Burger

Prep Time: 5 minutes

Cook Time: 25 minutes

Servings: 6

INGREDIENTS

24 oz (1.5 lbs) ground turkey

18 slices nitrate-free bacon

2 medium tomatoes

6 large romaine lettuce leaves

1/2 teaspoon paprika (or smoked or Hungarian paprika)

1/2 teaspoon ground black pepper

1 teaspoon Celtic sea salt

INSTRUCTIONS

1. Heat large pan or skillet over medium heat.
2. Add bacon to hot pan or skillet. Cook about 5 - 6 minutes on each side, until browned and crisp. Flip halfway through cooking. Set aside on paper towel to drain. Reserve 4 tablespoons bacon fat in pan. Reserve remaining bacon fat for later use.
3. Add ground turkey, 1 tablespoon bacon fat, salt and spices to medium mixing bowl. Mix well with hands or large wooden spoon.
4. Form turkey mixture into 6 patties and add to hot oiled pan. Cook about 4 - 5 minutes on each side, for medium doneness. Flip halfway through cooking.
5. Remove burgers from pan and drain on paper towels.

6. Slice tomatoes. Lay lettuce leaves flat. Place burger patties on one end of lettuce and top with bacon and tomato slices. Wrap up burger in lettuce. Repeat with remaining burgers, bacon and veggies.
7. Transfer to serving dish and serve immediately.

Apple Cinnamon Waffles

Cook Time: 15 minutes

Servings: 2

INGREDIENTS

1 cup almond flour

1/2 cup coconut flour

1 small apple (sweet or tart)

3 cage-free eggs (separated)

2 tablespoons coconut oil

2 - 4 tablespoons stevia

1 tablespoon aluminum-free baking soda

1 teaspoon vanilla

1 teaspoon ground cinnamon

1/4 teaspoon sea salt

Coconut oil (for cooking)

INSTRUCTIONS

1. Preheat waffle iron. Use wadded paper towel or grill brush to carefully coat cooking surface with coconut oil. Heat medium pan over medium-high heat. Lightly coat pan with coconut oil.
2. In medium mixing bowl, beat egg whites to medium-stiff peaks with hand mixer, about 5 minutes. Or stand mixer, about 3 minutes.

3. In large mixing bowl, beat together egg yolks, oil, stevia, vanilla and cinnamon with hand mixer or whisk. Grate or finely dice apple and add to egg mixture.
4. In small mixing bowl, combine flours, salt and baking soda. Beat flour mixture into egg yolk and apple mixture. Gently fold egg whites into batter.
5. Pour portion of batter onto hot waffle iron. Do not overfill. Cook 4 - 5 minutes, until golden brown and crisp. Set aside cooked *Waffles*. Repeat with remaining batter. Coat waffle iron with more coconut oil, if necessary.
6. Transfer *Waffles* to wire rack to cool completely. Once cooled, place in airtight container and store in freezer. Place small parchment sheets in between waffles, if desired.
7. To serve, place pancakes in toaster, toaster oven or preheated oven and cook until heated through. Serve with topping of choice.

Kelp Noodle Stir-Fry

Prep Time: 10 minutes

Cook Time: 10 minutes

Servings: 2

INSTRUCTIONS

1 (12 oz) package kelp noodles

8 oz grass-fed beef

1/2 sweet onion

1 red bell pepper

1 hot chili pepper

2 cloves garlic

1 inch piece fresh ginger

1/2 teaspoon paprika

1/2 teaspoon ground black pepper

1/4 teaspoon sea salt

Small bunch fresh cilantro

1 lime

Coconut oil (for cooking)

DIRECTIONS

1. Heat large skillet or medium cast-iron wok over high heat. Drain and rinse kelp noodles. Add to medium bowl and soak for 5 minutes in water and juice of 1/2 lime.
2. Stem and seed peppers. Peel onion, garlic and ginger. Dice beef into strips and add to medium mixing bowl. Mince chili pepper,

garlic and ginger. Add to beef with salt, pepper, paprika and 1 teaspoon coconut oil. Mix with wooden spoon to evenly coat beef.
3. Slice onion and bell pepper and add to hot skillet. Sauté about 2 minutes. Add seasoned beef to skillet and sauté another 2 minutes to brown.
4. Drain kelp noodles and add to skillet. Stir until beef is browned and cooked to about medium-well, kelp noodles are heated through, and veggies caramelize.
5. Remove skillet from heat and plate stir-fry. Chop fresh cilantro.
6. Top stir-fry with cilantro and squeeze of 1/2 lime.
7. Serve hot.

Quick Beanless Chili

Prep Time: 5 minutes

Cook Time: 20 minutes

Servings: 4

INGREDIENTS

1 lb lean grass-fed ground beef (or elk, bison, turkey or chicken)

15 oz (1 can) organic tomato sauce

6 oz (1 can) organic tomato paste

1 small onion

1 bell pepper

2 cloves garlic

2 tablespoons chili powder

1 tablespoon ground cumin

1 tablespoon smoked paprika (or paprika)

1 teaspoon Mexican oregano (or dried oregano)

1 teaspoon ground black pepper

1 teaspoon sea salt

1/2 teaspoon cayenne pepper

1 tablespoon coconut oil

sea salt, to taste

INSTRUCTIONS

1. Heat medium pot over medium-high heat. Add 1 tablespoon coconut oil.

2. Peel onion and garlic. Stem and seed bell pepper. Chop and add to food processor or bullet blender. Pulse until finely minced.
3. Add to skillet and sauté for about 1 minute. Add ground beef and spices. Brown beef for about 5 minutes. Stir with whisk to break up meat well, or wooden spoon to keep beef chunkier.
4. Add whole cans of tomato sauce and paste. Stir to combine.
5. Bring to a simmer, then reduce heat to medium and cover loosely with lid to prevent splatter. Simmer about 10 minutes. Stir occasionally.
6. Use large serving spoon or ladle to serve hot.

Macadamia Crusted Ahi Tuna

Prep Time: 5 minutes

Cook Time: 1 minute

Servings: 1

INGREDIENTS

8 oz ahi tuna fillet

1/4 teaspoon coconut oil

1/4 teaspoon dried thyme

1/4 teaspoon dried tarragon (optional)

1/4 cup whole macadamia nuts (shelled)

1 small garlic clove teaspoon

1 small shallot teaspoon

1/2 teaspoon ground white pepper (or black pepper)

1/2 teaspoon sea salt

2 tablespoons coconut oil

INSTRUCTIONS

1. Heat medium pan over medium-high heat. Add 2 tablespoons coconut oil to pan.
2. Chop macadamia nuts well. Peel and finely mince garlic and shallot. Set aside.
3. Rub top and bottom of fillet with 1/4 teaspoon coconut oil, salt, pepper, thyme and tarragon (optional).
4. Press 1/2 chopped macadamia nuts into each side of fillet.

5. Add garlic and shallots to hot oiled pan and sauté for just a second. Do not burn.
6. Carefully place fish in pan and sear 15 - 30 seconds on each side, for rare to medium rare. Carefully flip half way through cooking.
7. Transfer fillet to serving dish and serve hot with mixed greens or favorite veggies.

Parchment Baked Salmon

Prep Time: 5 minutes

Cook Time: 20 minutes

Servings: 1

INGREDIENTS

8 oz salmon fillet (deboned, skin-on)

6 - 8 medium asparagus stalks

1/2 lemon

1 basil sprig

1 rosemary sprig

1 teaspoon coconut oil

Pinch black pepper

Pinch sea salt

Parchment paper

Kitchen twine

INSTRUCTIONS

1. Place large sheet pan on bottom rack of oven. Preheat oven to 400 degrees F. prepare parchment sheet.
2. Place salmon in middle of parchment sheet skin-side down and sprinkle with salt and pepper. Place asparagus stalks next to salmon. Cut lemon into thin slices and place over fish and asparagus. Rub herbs between palms, then lay basil and rosemary sprig over lemon slices. Drizzle 1 teaspoon coconut oil over salmon and asparagus.

3. Gather edges of parchment up over salmon and tie tightly with kitchen twine to form sealed pouch.
4. Place pouch directly on hot baking sheet in hot oven. Bake for 20 minutes.
5. Remove from oven and carefully transfer pouch to serving plate. Carefully open pouch to release steam.
6. Serve hot.

Seafood Paella

Prep Time: 10 minutes

Cook Time: 25 minutes

Servings: 4

INGREDIENTS

1 large head cauliflower

8 oz natural sausage, cooked

8 oz large shrimp

12 live little neck clams

12 live mussels

4 bone-in chicken thighs

1 cup chicken stock (or seafood stock)

1 small white onion

2 tablespoons smoked paprika

1 teaspoon saffron

Pinch ground black pepper

Pinch sea salt

2 tablespoons coconut oil

INSTRUCTIONS

1. Heat large pan over medium heat and add coconut oil.
2. Peel and chop onion. Add to hot oiled pan and sauté until translucent, about 2 minutes.
3. Add chicken thighs and brown about 5 minutes. Turn chicken over and cook another 5 minutes.

4. Rinse and clean clams and mussels, and remove any beards with pliers. Peel and devein shrimp. Cut sausage into 1 inch slices. Set aside.
5. Roughly chop cauliflower and add to food processor with shredding attachment, process to "rice." Or mince cauliflower with knife.
6. Add riced or minced cauliflower to chicken and sauté 2 minutes. Add sausage, clams, mussels and shrimp. Add paprika and saffron and sauté another 2 minutes.
7. Add chicken or seafood stock and stir to combine. Increase heat to high and bring to simmer. Reduce heat to medium-high and cover. Let simmer about 5 - 7 minutes, until liquid evaporates, shrimp is opaque, and mussels and clams open. Discard any that do not open.
8. Plate and serve hot.

Zucchini Salad with Sundried Tomato Sauce

Prep Time: 20 minutes*

Servings: 2

INGREDIENTS

1 medium zucchini

1 tomato

5 sundried tomatoes

1 garlic clove

2 fresh basil leaves

1 tablespoon raw virgin coconut oil (or 2 tablespoons warm water)

1/4 teaspoon ground white pepper (or black pepper)

1/4 teaspoon sea salt

INSTRUCTIONS

1. Run zucchini through spiralizer, slice into long, thin shreds with knife, or use vegetable peeler to make flat, thin slices. Sprinkle with a pinch of salt and pepper, and gently toss to coat.
2. Add tomato, sundried tomatoes, peeled garlic, basil, coconut oil or warm water, and remaining salt and pepper to food processor or bullet blender. Process until sauce of desired consistency forms.
3. Transfer zucchini pasta to serving bowls. Top with tomato sauce and serve immediately.
4. Or refrigerate for 20 minutes and serve chilled.

Cashew Crunch Kelp Noodle Salad

Prep Time: 10 minutes*

Servings: 2

INGREDIENTS

1 package (12 oz) kelp noodles

1/2 lemon

1/2 small red bell pepper

Cashew Sauce

1 cup raw cashews

1/2 small red bell pepper

1/2 lemon

1 tablespoon coconut aminos (or raw apple cider vinegar)

2 large basil leaves

1/2 teaspoon smoked paprika

1/2 teaspoon ground black pepper

1/2 teaspoon Celtic sea salt

1/4 teaspoon ground turmeric (optional)

1/4 teaspoon smoked chili powder (optional)

Water

INSTRUCTIONS

1. *Soak 3/4 cup cashews in enough water to cover at least 4 hours, or overnight in refrigerator. Drain and rinse.

2. Drain and rinse kelp noodles. Add to medium bowl with warm water and juice of 1/2 lemon. Set aside 5 minutes.
3. Cut bell pepper in half. Remove stem, seeds and veins and set half of pepper aside. Julienne (thinly slice) remaining bell pepper and add to medium mixing bowl.
1. For *Crunchy Cashew Sauce*, add soaked cashews, bell pepper, juice of 1/2 lemon, coconut aminos, basil, salt and spices to food processor or high-speed blender. Process until smooth, about 2 minutes. Add enough water to reach desired consistency. Set aside.
4. Drain kelp noodles and add to sliced bell pepper. Add *Cashew Sauce* and toss to coat. Transfer noodles to serving dishes.
5. Roughly chop remaining 1/4 cup cashews. Sprinkle noodles and serve immediately. Or refrigerate for 20 minutes and serve chilled.

Raspberry Almond Salad

Prep Time: 10 minutes

Servings: 1

INGREDIENTS

Salad

2 cups soft lettuce leaves (looseleaf or butterhead varieties)

1/2 cup watercress

2 tablespoons raw almonds (slivered or sliced)

1/4 cup fresh raspberries

Raspberry Vinaigrette

1/4 cup raspberries (fresh or frozen)

2 tablespoons lemon juice (or raw apple cider vinegar)

2 tablespoons raw walnuts (or raw walnut oil, coconut oil, almond oil, etc.)

1 teaspoon stevia (optional)

Water

INSTRUCTIONS

1. For *Salad*, rinse, dry and plate lettuce and watercress. Sprinkle almonds and fresh raspberries over greens.
2. For *Raspberry Vinaigrette*, add raspberries, lemon juice, walnuts or oil, and stevia (optional) to food processor or high-speed blender and process until smooth, about 1 minute. Add enough water to reach desired consistency.

3. Drizzle *Raspberry Vinaigrette* over salad and serve immediately.

Healthy Chicken Satay

Prep Time: 10 minutes*

Cook Time: 25 minutes

Servings: 4

INGREDIENTS

16 oz (1 lb) boneless skinless chicken

12 wooden skewers (soaked in water for 1 hour)

Marinade

1 tablespoon pure fish sauce (or liquid aminos or coconut Aminos)

2 inch piece fresh ginger rot

1 garlic clove

Satay Sauce

13 oz (1 can) light coconut milk

1/2 cup crunchy almond butter

1 tablespoon stevia

1 tablespoon pure fish sauce (or tamari or coconut aminos)

1 teaspoon apple cider vinegar (or liquid aminos or coconut vinegar)

4 shallots

2 garlic cloves

2 inch piece fresh ginger root

2 small red chili peppers

1 1/2 tablespoons lime juice

Coconut oil (for cooking)

INSTRUCTIONS

1. *Cut chicken into 1 inch strips. For *Marinade*, peel and mince garlic and ginger. Add to medium mixing bowl with fish sauce and whisk. Add chicken and toss with until coated. Cover and set aside to marinate for 1 hour.
2. *Soak wooden skewers in water in shallow dish for 1 hour.
3. Heat medium pan or wok over medium heat and add 1 tablespoon coconut oil.
4. For *Satay Sauce*, peel and mince shallots, garlic and ginger. Slice peppers. Add to hot pan and sauté until softened, about 5 - 8 minutes.
5. Reduce heat to low. Add almond butter, coconut milk, stevia, fish sauce, vinegar and lime juice. Whisk until blended. Gently simmer for 10 minutes. Remove from heat, but keep warm.
6. Preheat outdoor grill or griddle pan over medium-high heat. Lightly coat with coconut oil.
7. Pierce marinated chicken strips with soaked skewers. Pour some *Satay Sauce* over chicken and brush lightly with marinade brush to coat. Transfer remaining *Satay Sauce* to serving dish.
8. Grill chicken on preheated grill until just cooked through, about 3 minutes per side. Turn over skewers halfway through cooking. Do not overcook.
9. Remove skewers from heat and transfer to serving dish. Serve with *Satay Sauce*.

Oven-Fried Chicken

Prep Time: 10 minutes

Cook Time: 60 minutes

Servings: 4

INGREDIENTS

32 oz (2 lb) bone-in, skinless chicken

3/4 cup fine almond flour

3/4 cup coarse almond meal (or almond flour)

2 cage free eggs

1/3 cup nut milk

1/2 teaspoon cayenne pepper

1 teaspoon ground black pepper

1 1/2 teaspoons paprika

1 1/2 tablespoons Celtic sea salt

Coconut oil (in spray bottle)

INSTRUCTIONS

1. Preheat oven to 350 degrees F. Fill spray bottle with warm coconut oil.
2. Line sheet pan with aluminum foil. Place metal cooling or baking rack over lined sheet pan. Generously spray metal rack with coconut oil to coat. Set second sheet pan aside.
3. Add almond meal and/or flour to small mixing bowl with 1 tablespoon salt and spices. Mix to combine with fork or whisk to break up clumps.

4. In shallow dish, beat eggs and nut milk until combined.
5. Use serving spoon or measuring cup to dust second sheet pan with layer of almond flour mixture onto. Sprinkle chicken with 1/2 tablespoon salt.
6. Dip and coat all chicken pieces in egg mixture then lay on second sheet pan, over layer of almond flour mixture. Use spoon or measuring cut to sprinkle almond flour mixture from mixing bowl over dipped chicken. Pat almond flour mixture into chicken on all sides until well coated.
7. Transfer coasted chicken to prepared wire rack. Generously spray coated chicken with coconut oil.
8. Bake 60 - 70 minutes, until coating is crisp and chicken is cooked through. Remove from oven and allow to cool at least 10 minutes. Then place crispy chicken on paper towels to drain, if desired.
9. Transfer to serving dish and serve immediately.

Baked Egg Muffins

Prep time: 5 minutes

Cook time: 15-20 minutes

INGREDIENTS

1 tbsp olive oil

1 tbsp coconut oil

6 cage-free eggs

1 onion

½ yellow bell pepper

½ red bell pepper

¼ tsp ground black pepper

¼ tsp Celtic sea salt

INSTRUCTIONS

1. Preheat oven to 350. Whisk all 6 eggs in a bowl. Chop the onion and bell pepper into small pieces.
2. In a pan, combine olive oil with onion over medium-high heat for 2 minutes. Add peppers and cook another 2 minutes.
3. Remove onion/peppers from heat and let cool a few minutes. Combine them with the eggs. Add the Celtic sea salt and ground black pepper and mix.
4. Coat a muffin pan with the coconut oil. Fill each muffin cup with the egg/pepper/onion mix. Do not fill a muffin cup more than ¾ full.

5. Place the pan in the oven and bake 10-15 minutes, removing the pan from the oven when the tops of the muffins get fluffy and golden brown.
6. Remove the muffins from the pan and serve.

Spicy Kale with Poached Eggs

Prep time: 10 minutes

Cook time: 12 minutes

INGREDIENTS

1 handful kale

2 cage-free eggs

1 small onion

1 clove garlic

1 tbsp extra virgin olive oil

¼ tsp ground black pepper

1 tsp low-sodium horseradish (optional)

INSTRUCTIONS

1. Chop the onion and mince the garlic. De-stem and wash the kale. Leaving a bit of water on the kale is ideal.
2. In a saucepan, add 1 tbsp extra virgin olive oil over medium heat. Add onion and cook until it begins to lose its opaqueness, about 5 minutes.
3. Add kale to saucepan and cover until kale is soft and green, about 5 minutes. Add garlic and stir, then cook another 2 minutes and remove from heat.
4. Fill a saucepan half full of water. Bring the water to a boil, then reduce heat below a boil and hold it there.
5. One by one, crack the eggs into a small cup or bowl and, with the lip of the cup or bowl close to the water's surface, dump the egg

into the water. If necessary, nudge the eggwhites closer to the yolks to keep them together.

6. Once all the eggs are in the water, remove the pan from heat and cover it. Let sit for 4 minutes until all eggs are cooked, then remove eggs from pan.
7. Place the greens on a plate and the two eggs on top of the greens. Top with horseradish if desired. Serve.

Spicy Oregano Cubes

Prep time: 1 hr 10 minutes

Cook time: 16-20 minutes

Serves: 4

INGREDIENTS

1 boneless leg of lamb

5 tbsp extra virgin olive oil

2 tsp dried oregano

1 tbsp fresh parsley

1 lemon

½ eggplant

4 small onions

2 tomatoes

5 fresh bay leaves

¼ tsp Celtic sea salt

¼ tsp ground black pepper

INSTRUCTIONS

1. Cube the lamb, chop the fresh parsley, juice the lemon, slice and quarter the eggplant into thick pieces, halve the onions and quarter the tomatoes.

2. Place lamb in a bowl. Mix olive oil, oregano, parsley, lemon juice and Celtic sea salt and ground black pepper. Pour this over the lamb and mix well. Cover and marinate for 1 hour.
3. Preheat the grill. Thread the marinated lamb, eggplant, onions, tomatoes and bay leaves in evenly on each of four skewers.
4. Place the kebabs on a grill inside a grill pan and brush them evenly with the leftover marinade until the marinade is all gone. Cook over medium heat turning once the kebabs once, for about 8-10 minutes on each side, basting them whenever enough juice collects in the bottom of the grill pan.
5. Serve immediately or chill 20 minutes and then serve.

Red Pepper Chicken Fries

Prep time: 10 minutes

Cook time: 12 minutes

Serves: 4

INGREDIENTS

4 pieces grass-fed chicken thighs

1 large red pepper

1 large yellow pepper

1 large orange pepper

1 onion

1 clove garlic

1 tbsp coconut oil

¼ tsp ground black pepper

¼ tsp chinese five spice

INSTRUCTIONS

1. Chop the chicken into small cubes, about 1" each. Chop the peppers and onion into ½" cubes. Mince garlic.
2. In a pan, combine coconut oil with peppers and onion and cook over medium heat for 4 minutes.

3. Add chicken, pepper, chinese five spice, and stir, cooking 4 more minutes.
4. Flip and mix well (in order to cook chicken evenly), add garlic, and cook for 4 more minutes, or until chicken is cooked through.
5. Serve immediately or chill 20 minutes and then serve.

Chicken Bruschetta

Prep time: 10 minutes

Cook time: 10 minutes

Serves: 4

INGREDIENTS

4 grass-fed chicken breasts

2 tomatoes

4 olives

2 onions

¼ tsp ground black pepper

1 cup roasted red pepper

3 tbsp extra virgin olive oil

INSTRUCTIONS

1. Dice the tomatoes, chop the olives and onions, and combine them with ground black pepper and 2 tbsp olive oil in a bowl and mix well into a bruschetta. Puree the roasted red pepper in a blender and set aside.
2. Combine the chicken with 1 tbsp extra virgin olive oil and cook in a pan over medium-high heat for 4 minutes, turn once, and cook another 4-6 minutes, removing from heat while still tender.

3. Place one piece of chicken on each plate and pour the roasted red pepper over each, adding bruschetta over the top. Garnish with basil and serve.

Salmon with Berry Chutney

Prep time: 10 minutes

Cook time: 15 minutes

Serves: 4

INGREDIENTS

4 salmon filets

16 stalks of asparagus

1 cup blueberries

1 onion

1 clove garlic

1 tbsp ginger root

¼ cup apple cider vinegar

½ tsp cinnamon

INSTRUCTIONS

1. Preheat your broiler. Finely chop the onion, garlic and ginger. Prepare a stove-top pot to steam the asparagus.
2. Combine blueberry, onion, garlic, ginger, apple cider vinegar and cinnamon in a saucepan and bring to a simmer, stirring continuously. Remove from heat once it has thickened into a sauce and set aside to cool.

3. Steam the asparagus for 3-5 minutes and broil the fish for 5-7 minutes. Remove from oven.
4. Lay one piece of fish across each plate and pour the blueberry chutney over top. Lay 4 stalks of asparagus over each piece of fish and serve.

Baked Tilapia Filets

Prep time: 10 minutes

Cook time: 15 minutes

Serves: 4

INGREDIENTS

4 filets of tilapia

¼ tsp chipotle chili pepper powder

1 lemon

1 cup coconut milk

1 clove garlic

1 tsp lemon juice

2 tbsp dill

¼ tsp black ground pepper

INSTRUCTIONS

1. Preheat oven to 350 degrees. Chop the garlic and the dill and cut the lemon into slices.
2. Season tilapia with chipotle chili pepper powder and black ground pepper. Bake for 15 minutes or until tilapia flakes with a fork.
3. Combine coconut milk, garlic, lemon juice and dill in a bowl.

4. Remove fish from oven and pour sauce over the top, placing a lemon wedge over each. Serve immediately or chill 20 minutes and then serve.

Mushroom Masala

Prep Time: 10 minutes

Cook Time: 25 minutes

Servings: 8

INGREDIENTS

1 head cauliflower

1 1/2 cups tomato purée (or tomato sauce)

1 pint (2 cups) mushrooms

1 onion

1 chili pepper

1 /2 green bell pepper

1 large garlic clove

1 inch piece fresh ginger

2 teaspoons coriander leaves (optional)

1 teaspoon garam masala

1/2 teaspoon cayenne pepper

1/2 teaspoon ground coriander

1/2 teaspoon Celtic sea salt

3 tablespoons coconut oil

INSTRUCTIONS

1. Roughly chop cauliflower, then rice cauliflower in food processor, or mince. Add to medium pot with enough water to cover. Heat pot over medium heat and cook until just tender, about 8 minutes. Drain and transfer to serving dish.

2. Heat medium pan over medium heat. Add coconut oil to hot pan.
3. Peel and finely dice onions. Remove seeds, veins and stem from bell pepper and dice. Slice chili pepper. Peel and mince garlic and onion. Add to hot oiled pan and sauté about 5 minutes.
4. Slice mushrooms and add to pan with tomato, salt and spices. Finely chop coriander leaves and add to pan (optional). Sauté and let simmer about 10 - 12 minutes, stirring occasionally.
5. Transfer to serving dish and serve hot with cauliflower rice.

Ground Beef Stuffed Peppers

Prep Time: 10 minutes

Cook Time: 50 minutes

Servings: 4

INGREDIENTS

4 bell peppers

16 oz (1 lb) ground meat (beef, pork, chicken, turkey, etc.)

1/2 head cauliflower (1 cup riced)

1/2 cup roasted red peppers

1/4 cup sundried tomatoes

1/4 cup pecans

1/2 small onion (white, yellow or red)

2 tablespoons coconut oil

2 garlic cloves

Medium bunch fresh herbs (parsley, oregano, thyme, etc.)

1/4 teaspoon red pepper flakes

1 teaspoon ground white pepper (or black pepper)

1 teaspoon Celtic sea salt

Water

INSTRUCTIONS

1. Preheat oven to 350 degrees F.
2. Cut tops off peppers, then remove stems from tops and seeds and veins from bottoms of peppers. Leave bottoms of peppers hollow

but do not pierce. Place in baking dish just large enough to fit peppers snuggly. Set aside.
3. Peel onion and garlic. Roughly chop onions, garlic and cauliflower. Add to food processor or high-speed blender with pecans. Pulse about 15 seconds.
4. Add tops of peppers, roasted red peppers, sundried tomatoes, ground meat, salt, pepper, and fresh herbs to processor. Process until coarsely ground, about 1 - 2 minutes.
5. Use large spoon to stuff peppers with mixture. Add 1/2 cup water to bottom of baking dish. Cover peppers with aluminum foil.
6. Bake 30 minutes. Carefully remove foil and continue baking uncovered 10 - 20 minutes, until stuffing is golden brown and cooked through .
7. Carefully remove from oven and transfer peppers to serving dish. Serve hot.

Chicken Souvlaki Kebobs

Prep Time: 5 minutes*

Cook Time: 15 minutes

Servings: 4

INGREDIENTS

12 oz (3/4 lb) boneless skinless chicken

1 lemon

2 garlic cloves

1/2 small white onion

1/2 yellow bell pepper

1/2 cup grape tomato

1 teaspoon dried oregano

3/4 teaspoon Celtic sea salt

2 tablespoons coconut oil

8 skewers

INSTRUCTIONS

1. *Soak wooden skewers in water for 10 minutes, if using.
2. Juice lemon into medium mixing bowl. Peel and mince garlic. Remove stem, seeds and veins from bell pepper. Peel onion. Roughly chop pepper and onion. Add to bowl with tomatoes, 1 tablespoon coconut oil, oregano and salt.
3. *Pierce chicken multiple times with fork, then cut into one inch chunks. Add to bowl and mix to combine. Let set aside in refrigerator for 10 minutes.

4. Heat small skillet or griddle over medium-high heat and add 1 tablespoon coconut oil.
5. Drain marinated chicken and veggies, then carefully add to skewer, alternating meat and veggies.
6. Add chicken and veggie skewer to hot oiled skillet or griddle. Grill for about 1 - 2 minutes then turn 1/4 the way around. Continue cooking and turning until chicken is golden brown and cooked through.
7. Remove from heat and serve immediately.

Homestyle Meatloaf

Prep Time: 10 minutes

Cook Time: 1 hour

Servings: 8

INGREDIENTS

Meatloaf

32 oz (2 lb) ground meat (beef, pork, turkey, chicken, or any combination)

3/4 cup almond flour

2 cage-free eggs

1 medium onion (white, yellow or red)

2 garlic cloves

2 tablespoons oregano

2 tablespoons paprika

1 tablespoon dried thyme

1 tablespoon ground bay leaf (optional)

1 tablespoon ground black pepper

Ketchup

6 oz (1 can) organic tomato paste

3/4 cup water

1 tablespoon apple cider vinegar

1/4 teaspoon garlic powder

1/4 teaspoon onion powder

Pinch all spice (optional)

INSTRUCTIONS

1. Preheat oven to 350 degrees F. Heat small pot over medium heat.
2. For *Ketchup*, add tomato paste, water, apple cider vinegar, garlic powder, onion powder and all spice (optional) to small pot. Reduced for about 5 minutes, stirring occasionally. Remove from heat and set aside.
3. For *Meatloaf*, peel and mince garlic and onion. Or add to food processor and coarsely grind. Add to large mixing bowl.
4. Add eggs to mixing bowl and mix lightly. Add ground meat, almond flour, spices and salt. Mix with hands or large wooden spoon until well combined.
5. Spread a few spoonfuls of *Ketchup* into bottom of medium loaf pan. Transfer meat mixture to loaf pan. Pack slightly and smooth top. Spread 1/2 of *Ketchup* over top of Meatloaf. Cover with aluminum foil and bake for 30 minutes.
6. Carefully remove *Meatloaf* from oven and remove foil. Spread remaining ketchup over *Meatloaf* and continue to bake uncovered for 15 - 30 minutes, until meatloaf is cooked through and Ketchup is caramelized.
7. Remove from oven and let Meatloaf rest about 5 - 10 minutes.
8. Use large spatulas to remove whole *Meatloaf* from pan. Or leave *Meatloaf* in pan, and slice and serve warm.

Asian Empanada

Prep Time: 20 minutes

Cook Time: 20 minutes

Servings: 4

INSTRUCTIONS

Crust

1 cup almond flour

1 cup coconut flour

2 eggs

3 tablespoons sesame oil (or coconut oil)

1/2 teaspoon garlic powder

1/2 teaspoon onion powder

1/2 teaspoon ground ginger

1/4 teaspoon baking soda

1 teaspoon sea salt

1 tablespoon sesame oil (or coconut oil)

1 tablespoon sesame seeds

Filling

6 oz chicken or shrimp

1/2 head cabbage (1 cup shredded)

1/4 cup mushrooms

2 inch piece fresh ginger

2 garlic cloves

1 tablespoon pure fish sauce

1 teaspoon apple cider vinegar

1 shallot

1 scallion

1 teaspoon sesame oil

DIRECTIONS
1. For *Crust*, sift almond and coconut flour into medium mixing bowl. Add baking soda, spices and salt.
2. Whisk eggs in small mixing bowl, then add to flour and combine. Slowly add 3 tablespoons oil until malleable dough comes together.
3. Roll in plastic wrap or wrap tightly in parchment and refrigerate for 15 minutes.
4. Preheat oven to 400 degrees. Line sheet pan with parchment or baking mat. Cover cutting board with parchment. Het medium pan over medium heat.
5. Shred cabbage and slice mushrooms. Peel and grate ginger. Slice scallion. Peel and mince shallot and garlic. Dice chicken or slice shrimp in half.
6. Add sesame oil to pan. Add chicken or shrimp hot oiled pan with ginger, shallot and garlic. Sauté about 90 seconds. Add cabbage and mushrooms and sauté for a minute.
7. Add vinegar and fish sauce. Sauté about 3 minutes until cabbage is wilted. Stir in scallions. Remove from heat and set aside.
8. Remove dough from refrigerator. Divide dough into 4 portions. Roll dough into balls and flatten on parchment covered cutting board with hands. Roll into circles about 1/8 inch thick with rolling pin.

9. Scoop equal portions of *Filling* into center of one side of dough circle. Fold bare half of dough over filled half. Press edges together, letting any trapped air escape. Crimp edges of dough together with fork. Repeat with remaining dough.
10. Bruch tops of empanada with sesame oil and sprinkle with sesame seeds.
11. Arrange empanadas on lined sheet pan and bake 15 - 20 minutes, or until dough is golden and cooked through.
12. Serve immediately. Or allow to cool and store in air-tight container.

Made in the USA
Middletown, DE
08 November 2020